SPANISH COOKING

GALLERY BOOKS
An Imprint of W. H. Smith Publishers Inc.
112 Madison Avenue
New York City 10016

INTRODUCTION

Spanish cuisine has been a very well kept secret for a long time, and it is only recently that people have begun to discover that there is a lot to like about Spanish food, and that the old myths about the food being fiery-hot and very oily are untrue. While the food is flavorful, this comes mostly from a subtle blend of herbs and spices rather then a heavy-handed use of chili peppers. Olive oil is the usual choice for frying, sautéeing and salad dressing, but there is no oil more fragrant.

Spanish cuisine is made up of foods that most of us know and like, and ones that are easy to find. It is the different combinations of those familiar ingredients that truly reflect Spanish flavor.

Although the style of eating in Spain is evolving just as it is everywhere else, and food is getting lighter, it still maintains a connection with culinary tradition. The recipes we have included reflect both the traditions and the new trends that make up the best of Spanish cuisine.

SERVES 6-8

GAZPACHO

A typically Spanish soup, this is the
perfect summer first course. The recipe
comes from Andalusia, in southern Spain.

1 medium green pepper, seeded and roughly chopped
8 medium tomatoes, peeled, seeded and roughly
    chopped
1 large cucumber, peeled and roughly chopped
1 large onion, roughly chopped
3-5oz French bread, crusts removed
3 tbsps red wine vinegar
3 cups water
Pinch salt and pepper
1-2 cloves garlic, crushed
3 tbsps olive oil
2 tsps tomato paste (optional)

Garnish

1 small onion, diced
½ small cucumber diced, but not peeled
3 tomatoes, peeled, seeded and diced
½ green pepper, seeded and diced

1. Combine all the prepared vegetables in a deep bowl
and add the bread, breaking it into small pieces by hand.
Mix together thoroughly.

2. Add the vinegar, water, salt, pepper and garlic.

3. Pour the mixture, a third at a time, into a blender or food
processor and purée for about 1 minute, or until the soup is
smooth.

4. Pour the purée into a clean bowl and gradually beat in
the olive oil using a whisk. Add enough tomato paste for a
good red color.

5. Cover the bowl tightly and refrigerate for at least 2 hours,
or until thoroughly chilled. Before serving, whisk the soup
to make sure all the ingredients are blended and then pour
into a large chilled soup tureen or into chilled individual
soup bowls. Serve all the garnishes in separate bowls to be
added to the soup if desired.

Step 2
Add the liquid,
seasoning and
garlic and stir the
mixture well.

Step 4
After puréeing the
soup, pour back
into a bowl and
whisk in the olive
oil by hand.

Cook's Notes

Time
Preparation takes about 20
minutes and the soup must
chill for at least 2 hours.

Preparation
Gazpacho may be prepared a
day in advance and kept
overnight in the refrigerator. To quickly
chill the soup, omit 1 cup water from the
recipe and use crushed ice instead.
Leave refrigerated for 30 minutes,
stirring frequently to melt the ice.

Variation
Use only enough garlic to suit
your own taste, or omit if
desired. Vary the garnishing
ingredients by using croûtons,
chopped green onions, or red onions,
red or yellow peppers.

SERVES 6

ANCHOVY STUFFED EGGS

A perfect 'tapa' or hors d'oeuvre with cocktails or
wine, these also make good picnic food.

6 eggs
6 anchovy fillets
½ fresh red chili, finely chopped
2 tsps finely chopped parsley or coriander
1 tbsp lemon juice
3-4 tbsps heavy cream
Salt
6 black olives, pitted

Step 3
Use the bowl of a
large spoon to roll
the eggs in the
hot water to set
the yolks in the
middle of the
whites.

Step 1
Use an egg
pricker or needle
to make a small
hole in the round-
ed end of each
egg to prevent
cracking.

Step 5
To fill the eggs,
use a small
teaspoon or a
pastry bag.

1. Prick the rounded end of each egg with a sharp needle
or an egg pricker. Lower the eggs carefully into boiling
water and bring back to the boil.

2. Using a large metal spoon, roll the eggs around in the
pan, gently, while the water comes up to the boil to set the
yolk in the middle of the white. Once the water is boiling,
allow the eggs to cook for about 9-10 minutes.

3. When the eggs are cooked, pour off the hot water and
rinse them under cold running water. Leave in the cold

water until ready for use.

4. Chop the anchovies finely and set them aside in a bowl.
When the eggs have cooled, peel them and cut them in half
lengthwise. Scoop out the yolks and add these to the
anchovies. Add all the remaining ingredients, except the
olives, and mix thoroughly. Do not over mix. The filling
should not be a uniform color.

5. Spoon or pipe the filling back into the hollow of each
egg white and top with half a black olive. Serve chilled.

Cook's Notes

 Time
Preparation takes about 20
minutes and cooking takes
9-10 minutes.

 Variation
Decorate the tops of the eggs
in various different ways. Use
stuffed green olives, small pieces of red
or green pepper or capers, for
example.

Serving Ideas
Serve as a tapa. The eggs are
also perfect for picnics.

SERVES 6

WHITE GAZPACHO

Often called Ajo Blanco, this soup is
prepared in much the same way as the
Gazpacho based on tomatoes.

6oz blanched almonds
1lb loaf white bread
1-2 cloves garlic, crushed
2 eggs
1 cup olive oil
½ cup white wine vinegar
Pinch of salt and white pepper
1 small bunch of seedless white grapes

Step 6
Beat the reserved
water into the
soup gradually.

Step 3
Purée the
almonds and the
garlic to form a
smooth paste.

Step 5
Squeeze the
bread to remove
all the water.

1. Place the almonds in a bowl and cover with boiling water. Leave to soak for about 30-45 minutes.

2. Cut the crusts from the bread and cut the bread into slices or cubes. Place in a bowl and cover with 4 cups cold water.

3. Drain the almonds and place them in a food processor or blender with the garlic. Process to a smooth paste.

4. Add the eggs and blend well. With the machine running, add the oil in a thin, steady stream.

5. Drain the bread, wringing it out with your hands, and reserve the water. Add the bread to the other ingredients in the food processor or blender and purée. Add vinegar, salt and white pepper and transfer the mixture to a bowl.

6. Gradually add the water, stirring constantly to the desired consistency. The soup should be as thick as light cream. Cover the soup and chill for at least 4 hours or overnight in the refrigerator. Garnish the soup with halved grapes to serve.

Cook's Notes

Time
Preparation takes about 25 minutes, with 4 hours minimum chilling time.

Variation
Use other light colored fruit such as melon, apples, pears or pineapple for garnish. Peeled cucumber, cut into small dice, may also be used. Vary the amount of garlic to suit your taste.

Cook's Tip
Be sure to add the oil in a thin, steady stream. If added too quickly, the soup may curdle. Adding extra bread will sometimes bring the mixture back together.

SERVES 4-6

TORTILLA
(SPANISH POTATO OMELET)

Unlike the usual French omelet, this
one isn't folded, so it's easier to prepare.

½ cup olive oil
½lb potatoes, peeled and thinly sliced
1 large onion, peeled and thinly sliced
Salt and pepper
4 eggs
2 tomatoes, peeled, seeded and roughly chopped or
    sliced
2 green onions, chopped

Step 4
Push the eggs
and potatoes
back from the
sides of the pan
using a fork.

Step 3
Pour the potato,
onion and egg
mixture into a
large frying pan.

Step 5
Slide pan under a
preheated broiler
to brown the top
of the omelet.

1. Heat the oil in a large frying pan and add the potatoes. Sprinkle lightly with salt and pepper and cook over medium heat until golden brown and crisp.

2. Add the onion once the potatoes begin to brown slightly. Turn the potatoes and onions over occasionally so that they brown evenly. They should take about 20 minutes to soften and brown.

3. Beat the eggs with a pinch of salt and pepper and stir the potatoes and onions into the eggs and pour the mixture back into the pan.

4. Cook over gentle heat until the bottom browns lightly.

5. Invert a large plate over the top of the pan and carefully turn the omelet out onto it.

6. Slide the omelet back into the pan so the uncooked side has a chance to brown. Cook until the eggs are set. Garnish with the tomatoes and green onions and serve warm.

Cook's Notes

Time
Preparation takes about 30 minutes, cooking takes about 30-40 minutes.

Preparation
As the potatoes cook, turn them frequently to prevent them sticking together. They will, however, stick slightly, which is not a problem.

Serving Ideas
The omelet may be cut into small squares and served as a tapa. It can also be served with a salad and bread for a light lunch or supper. Serve hot or cold.

SERVES 4

Avocado, Orange and Black Olive Salad

A light and colorful salad combining three of
Spain's abundant ingredients.

2 oranges, peeled and segmented
2 avocados
20 black olives, pitted
Basil leaves
½ small red onion, thinly sliced

Dressing

1 tbsp white wine or sherry vinegar
4 tbsps olive oil
½ tsp mustard
Pinch of salt and pepper

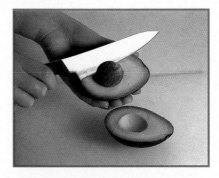

Step 1
Hit the stone with the sharp edge of a large knife and twist to remove it.

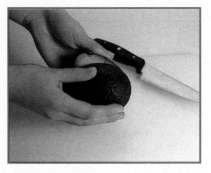

Step 1
Cut the avocados in half and twist to separate.

Step 1
To peel the avocado, lightly score the skin in two or three places, place the half cut side down on a chopping board and gently pull back the peel.

Use kitchen scissors to shred the basil leaves finely.

1. Make sure all the white pith is removed from each segment of orange. Cut the avocados in half and remove the stone. Peel them and cut into slices.

2. Cut the olives in half and slice them thinly or chop them.

3. Arrange the orange segments, avocado slices, sliced onion and olives on serving plates and sprinkle over the shredded basil leaves. Mix the dressing ingredients together well and pour over the salad to serve.

Cook's Notes

Time
Preparation takes about 30 minutes.

Cook's Tip
Do not peel the avocados more than 30 minutes before serving time unless you prepare the dressing beforehand and coat the avocados with it to prevent discoloration.

Variation
Green onions may be used instead of the red onions. Use different varieties of herbs. Substitute grapefruit for the orange.

SERVES 6

CARROT AND ZUCCHINI SALAD

This salad couldn't be easier. It is colorful, inexpensive and can be made almost all year round.

12oz carrots, peeled
12oz zucchini, topped and tailed
Grated rind and juice of 2 oranges
3 tbsps olive oil
Salt and pepper
4 tbsps unblanched almonds, chopped

Step 2
Grate the zucchini coarsely and add to the carrots.

Step 1
Grate the carrots on the coarse side of a grater.

Step 3
When grating oranges or other citrus fruit, use a pastry brush to remove all the zest from holes in grater.

1. Shred the carrots on the coarse side of a grater or use the coarse grating blade of a food processor. Place in a large bowl.

2. Grate the zucchini in the same way and add to the carrots.

3. Grate the orange on the fine side of the grater and then cut in half to squeeze the juice. Mix the juice and rind with the olive oil and salt and pepper. Pour over the carrots and the zucchini and stir well. Leave to marinate for about 15 minutes.

4. Sprinkle over the almonds and toss just before serving.

Cook's Notes

Time
Preparation takes about 15-25 minutes. Vegetables should marinate for about 15 minutes.

Preparation
The salad may be prepared in advance and left to stand longer than 15 minutes. Cover well and refrigerate.

Serving Ideas
Serve in individual bowls with a selection of other tapas. Spoon on to lettuce leaves for a first course or serve as a side salad.

SERVES 6

ROAST PEPPER SALAD

Charring the peppers makes the skins
easier to remove and gives a slightly
smoky taste that is very pleasant.

6 red peppers
6 tbsps olive oil
1 clove garlic, roughly chopped
2 tbsps red or white wine vinegar
Salt and pepper
1 green onion, diagonally sliced

Step 3
Broil the lightly-
oiled peppers
until the skins are
very charred.

Step 2
Flatten the
peppers by
pushing down
with the palm of
the hand.

Step 4
Use a small,
sharp knife to
peel away the
skin.

1. Preheat a broiler and cut the peppers in half, removing the seeds, stems and cores.

2. Flatten the peppers with the palm of your hand and brush the skin side of each pepper lightly with oil. Place the peppers under the broiler.

3. Broil the peppers until the skins are well charred on top. Do not turn the peppers over.

4. Wrap the peppers in a clean towel and leave to stand for about 15-20 minutes.

5. Unwrap the peppers and peel off the skin using a small, sharp knife. Cut the peppers into strips or into 1 inch pieces. Mix the remaining oil with the vinegar, salt and pepper. Place the peppers in a serving dish and pour over the dressing. Sprinkle over the garlic and green onion and leave the peppers to stand for about 30 minutes before serving.

Cook's Notes

Time
Preparation takes about 20 minutes. Broiling time for the peppers is approximately 10-12 minutes.

Preparation
The peppers must be well charred for the skin to loosen easily. Wrapping peppers in a tea towel creates steam, which helps to loosen the skin more easily.

Serving Ideas
Serve as a tapa or mix with cooked cold rice for a more substantial salad.

SERVES 4

SALMON AND VEGETABLE SALAD

The fish in this salad 'cooks' in the refrigerator in its vinegar marinade. Insist on very fresh fish for this recipe.

12oz salmon or salmon trout fillets
2 carrots, peeled and diced
1 large zucchini, peeled and diced
1 large turnip, peeled and diced
Chopped fresh coriander
3 tbsps tarragon or sherry vinegar
Salt and pepper
Pinch cayenne pepper
3 tbsps olive oil
Whole coriander leaves to garnish

Step 2
Cut all the vegetables into 1 inch dice.

Step 1
Place the salmon in a bowl with the vinegar and stir to coat well.

Step 3
When the salmon has marinated, it will become opaque and look cooked. Mix with the other ingredients.

1. Skin the salmon fillet and cut the fish into 1 inch pieces. Place in a bowl and add the vinegar, stirring well. Leave to stand for at least 2 hours.

2. Cut the vegetables into ½ inch dice and place the carrots in boiling water for about 5 minutes. Add the

zucchini and turnip during the last minute of cooking time.

3. Add the coriander, oil, salt and pepper and pinch cayenne pepper to the fish. Combine with the vegetables, mixing carefully so the fish does not break up. Chill briefly before serving, and garnish with coriander.

Cook's Notes

Time
Preparation takes about 30 minutes, with 2 hours for the salmon to marinate.

Cook's Tip
Fish allowed to marinate in vinegar, lemon or lime juice will appear opaque and 'cooked' after standing for about 2 hours.

Serving Ideas
Serve as a tapa or as a first course.

SERVES 6

FISH ESCABECH

Originally, this method of marinating sautéed fish in vinegar was simply a way of preserving it. All kinds of fish and even poultry and game were prepared this way.

3lb monkfish
6 tbsps flour
Pinch salt and pepper
1 medium carrot, peeled and thinly sliced
1 medium onion, thinly sliced
1 bay leaf
2 sprigs parsley
¼-½ fresh red chili, finely chopped
1½ cups white wine vinegar
6 cloves garlic, peeled and thinly sliced
Olive oil

1. Peel the brownish membrane from the outside of the monkfish tails.

2. Cut along the bone with a sharp filleting knife to separate the flesh from it.

3. Cut the monkfish into slices about 1 inch thick. Mix the salt and pepper with the flour and dredge the slices of monkfish, shaking off the excess. Fry in olive oil until golden brown. Remove and drain on paper towels.

4. Add the carrot and onion and fry gently for about 5 minutes. Add the bay leaf, parsley, vinegar, chili pepper and 1 cup water. Cover and simmer gently for about 20 minutes.

5. Place the fish in a shallow casserole dish and pour over the marinade. Sprinkle on the sliced garlic and cover well. Refrigerate for 24 hours, turning the fish over several times.

6. To serve, remove the fish from the marinade and arrange on a serving plate. Pour the marinade on top of the fish and garnish with parsley, if desired.

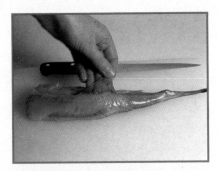

Step 1
Remove the brownish membrane from the outside of the monkfish tails.

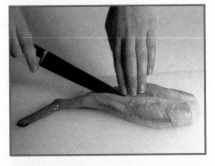

Step 2
Using a sharp filleting knife, cut along the bone to separate one side of the tail. Repeat with the other side.

Step 3
Slice the tails into 1 inch thick pieces.

Cook's Notes

 Time
Preparation takes about 25 minutes, with 24 hours refrigeration, cooking takes about 25 minutes.

 Variation
Other fish, such as whole small trout or trout fillets, or fish steaks such as cod or salmon, may be used.

 Serving Ideas
Serve as a first course or for a light lunch with a salad and bread.

SERVES 6

PAELLA

This dish has as many variations as Spain has cooks! Fish, meat and poultry combine with vegetables and rice to make a complete meal.

12 mussels in their shells
6 clams (if not available use 6 more mussels)
6oz cod, skinned and cut into 2 inch pieces
12 large shrimp
3 chorizos or other spicy sausage
2lb chicken cut in 12 serving-size pieces
1 small onion, chopped
1 clove garlic, crushed
2 small peppers, red and green, seeded and shredded
1lb long grain rice
Large pinch saffron
Salt and pepper
4 cups boiling water
5oz frozen peas
3 tomatoes, peeled, seeded and chopped or shredded

1. Scrub the clams and mussels well to remove beards and barnacles. Discard any with broken shells or those that do not close when tapped. Leave the mussels and clams to soak in water with a handful of flour for 30 minutes.

2. Remove the heads and legs from the shrimp, if desired, but leave on the tail shells.

3. Place the sausage in a saucepan and cover with water. Bring to the boil and then simmer for 5 minutes. Drain and slice into ¼ inch rounds. Set aside.

4. Heat the oil and fry the chicken pieces, browning evenly on both sides. Remove and drain on paper towels.

5. Add the sausage, onions, garlic and peppers to the oil in the frying pan and fry briskly for about 3 minutes.

6. Combine the sausage mixture with uncooked rice and saffron and place in a special Paella dish or a large oven-and flame-proof casserole. Pour on the water, season with salt and pepper and bring to the boil. Stir occasionally and allow to boil for about 2 minutes.

7. Add the chicken pieces and place in a preheated 400°F oven for about 15 minutes.

8. Add the clams, mussels, shrimp, cod and peas and cook a further 10-15 minutes or until the rice is tender, chicken is cooked and mussels and clams open. Discard any that do not open. Add the tomatoes 5 minutes before the end of cooking time and serve immediately.

Step 5
Cook the sausages, onions garlic and peppers briefly in oil.

Step 6
Combine the sausage mixture, rice and water in a special Paella dish or flame-proof casserole.

Cook's Notes

Time
Preparation takes about 30-40 minutes, cooking takes about 35-40 minutes.

Variation
Vary the ingredients to suit your own taste. Use other kinds of fish and shellfish. Omit chicken or substitute pork for part of the quantity. Use red or green onions if desired and add more sausage.

Watchpoint
Do not stir the Paella once it goes into the oven.

SERVES 4

MUSSELS IN RED WINE

Red wine makes an unusual, but very pleasant,
combination with seafood. This recipe is equally
good with clams or cockles.

3lb mussels, well scrubbed
1 cup dry red wine
6 tbsps olive oil
4 cloves garlic, finely chopped
2 bay leaves
2 tbsps fresh thyme, chopped
6 tbsps red wine vinegar
1 tsp paprika
Grated rind and juice of 1 lemon
Salt and pepper
Pinch cayenne pepper
Pinch sugar (optional)
Chopped parsley

Step 1
Cook the mussels over high heat, stirring frequently, until the shells begin to open.

1. Prepare the mussels as in the recipe for Paella. Place the wine in a large saucepan and bring to the boil. Add the mussels, cover the pan and cook briskly for about 4-5 minutes, stirring frequently, until the shells open. Discard any that do not open.

2. Transfer the mussels to a bowl and pour the cooking liquid through a fine strainer and reserve it.

Step 2
Transfer the mussels to a plate and pour the liquid through a fine strainer or through muslin.

3. In a clean saucepan, heat the oil and fry the garlic over gentle heat until golden brown. Add the bay leaves, thyme, vinegar, paprika, lemon juice and rind, salt, pepper and cayenne pepper. Pour on the wine, add sugar, if using, and bring to the boil. Cook to reduce to about ⅔ cup. Allow to cool completely.

4. Remove the mussels from their shells and add them to the liquid, stirring to coat all the mussels. Cover and place in the refrigerator for at least 2 hours. Allow to stand at room temperature for about 30 minutes before serving. Sprinkle with parsley.

Step 4
Remove the mussels from their shells with your fingers or by using a small teaspoon.

Cook's Notes

Time
Preparation takes about 30 minutes and cooking takes about 9-10 minutes.

Serving Ideas
Serve in small dishes as tapas. To serve as a more formal first course, place lettuce leaves on individual plates and spoon on the mussels. Sprinkle with chopped parsley, if desired.

Variation
Shelled mussels, purchased from a fishmonger, or frozen mussels may be used instead. If using frozen mussels, allow a further 2-3 minutes cooking time.

SERVES 4

BROILED FISH WITH ROMESCU

Romescu is a sauce that evolved from a fish stew recipe
and is still often considered a dish on its own. It is
simple to make and has a strong, pungent taste.

2lbs whole fish such as trout, red mullet, herring, sardines
or mackerel, allowing 1-4 fish per person, depending
on size.
Bay leaves
Salt and pepper
Olive oil
Lemon juice

Romescu (Almond and Hot Pepper Sauce)

1 tomato, peeled, seeded and chopped
3 tbsps ground almonds
½ clove garlic, crushed
½ tsp cayenne pepper
Pinch salt
3 tbsps red wine vinegar
⅔ cup olive oil

Step 1
Mix all the
ingredients
together into a
smooth paste
using a mortar
and pestle.

1. To prepare the sauce, combine all the ingredients,
except the olive oil and vinegar, in a mortar and pestle and
work to a smooth mixture.

2. Transfer to a bowl, whisk in red wine vinegar and add
the oil gradually, a few drops at a time, mixing vigorously
with a wire whisk or a wooden spoon. Make sure each
addition of oil is absorbed before adding more. Once about
half the oil is added, the remainder may be poured in in a
thin, steady stream. Adjust the seasoning and set the sauce
aside.

3. Wash the fish well, sprinkle the cavities with salt and
pepper and place in a bay leaf. Brush the skin with olive oil
and sprinkle with lemon juice. Place under a preheated
broiler and cook for about 2-5 minutes per side, depending
on the thickness of the fish. Brush with lemon juice and olive
oil while the fish is broiling. Serve with the sauce and lemon
or lime wedges if desired.

Step 2
Transfer the paste
to a bowl and
whisk in the wine
vinegar.

Step 2
Once half the oil
has been added,
add the remain-
der in a thin,
steady stream,
whisking by hand.

Cook's Notes

 Time
Preparation takes about 20
minutes and cooking takes
about 10-20 minutes.

 Preparation
The sauce may be made
several days in advance and
stored tightly sealed in the refrigerator.
Allow the sauce to come to room
temperature and whisk again before
serving.

 Serving Ideas
Serve with boiled or fried
potatoes and a salad.

SERVES 6

SEAFOOD STEW

This makes the most of the delicious
and varied fish and shellfish found
off Spain's beautiful coastline.

24 clams or mussels in the shell
3 squid
2lb firm whitefish, filleted into 2 inch pieces
3 medium-sized tomatoes, peeled, seeded and chopped
½ green pepper, seeded and chopped
1 small onion, chopped
1 clove garlic, finely chopped
1 cup dry white wine
Salt and pepper
½ cup olive oil
6 slices French bread
3 tbsps chopped parsley

1. Scrub the clams or mussels well to remove the beards and barnacles. Discard any shellfish with broken shells or ones that do not close when tapped. Place the mussels or clams in a large saucepan or heatproof casserole, scatter over about half of the vegetables and garlic and spoon over 4 tbsps of the olive oil.

2. To clean the squid, hold the tail section in one hand and the head section in the other to pull the tail away from the head.

3. Cut the tentacles free from the head just above the eyes. Discard the head, entrails and ink sack.

4. Remove the quill from the body of the squid and peel away the reddish-purple outer skin.

5. Slice the tail into strips about ½ inch thick. Cut the tentacles into individual pieces.

6. Scatter the squid and the prepared whitefish over the vegetables in the pan and top with the remaining vegetables. Pour over the white wine and season with salt and pepper. Bring to the boil over high heat and then reduce to simmering. Cover the pan and cook for about 20 minutes or until the clams open, the squid is tender and the fish flakes easily. Discard any clams or mussels that do not open.

7. Heat the remaining olive oil in a frying pan and when hot, add the slices of bread, browning them well on both sides. Drain on paper towels.

8. Place a slice of bread in the bottom of a soup bowl and ladle the fish mixture over the bread. Sprinkle with parsley and serve immediately.

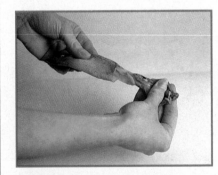

Step 2
To clean the squid, separate the head from the tail by pulling them in opposite directions

Step 4
Remove the quill from the tail and peel the reddish-purple skin from the outside.

Cook's Notes

 Time
Preparation takes about 35 minutes and cooking takes about 20 minutes.

Preparation
Fry the bread while the fish stew is cooking. The stew must be served immediately and not reheated.

Variation
Different kinds of fish, such as haddock, cod, halibut or sea bass can be used.

SERVES 4

MARINATED TROUT WITH EGG SAUCE

This recipe came from Navarre, an area famous for its brook trout.
The simply-prepared sauce allows the flavor of the fish to shine through.

4 even-sized trout, gutted but heads and tails left on
6 tbsps red wine
3 tbsps olive oil
3 tbsps water
1 clove garlic, crushed
2 sprigs fresh mint, 1 sprig fresh rosemary, 1 sprig fresh thyme, 1 small bay leaf, crumbled
6 black peppercorns
Pinch salt
3 egg yolks, lightly beaten
1 tbsp fresh herbs
Lemon or lime slices to garnish

1. Place the fish in a roasting pan and pour over the wine, oil, water and add the garlic and herbs. Sprinkle over the peppercorns and the salt and turn the fish several times to coat them thoroughly with the marinade. Leave at room temperature for about 30 minutes.

2. Place the roasting pan with the fish on top of the stove and bring the marinade just to the simmering point. Cover the pan and place in a preheated 350°F oven and cook for about 20 minutes or until the fish is firm.

3. Transfer the fish to a serving dish and peel off the skin on one side. Cover and keep warm.

4. Strain the fish cooking liquid into a bowl or the top of a double boiler and discard the herbs and garlic. Mix about 3 tbsps of the liquid into the egg yolks and then return to the bowl or double boiler.

5. Heat slowly, whisking constantly until the sauce thickens. Do not allow the sauce to boil. Add the chopped herbs and adjust the seasoning.

6. Coat the sauce over the skinned side of each trout and garnish the plate with lemon or lime wedges. Serve the rest of the sauce separately.

Step 2
Bring the marinade and fish to the simmering point on top of the stove. Allow to boil.

Step 3
When the fish is cooked, transfer to a serving dish and peel off one side of the skin on each fish.

Step 5
Cook the strained marinade and egg yolks slowly in a double boiler, whisking constantly until the sauce thickens.

Cook's Notes

Time
Preparation takes about 30 minutes, cooking takes about 20 minutes for the fish and about 5 minutes to finish the sauce.

Variation
The sauce may be made with white wine instead of red wine if desired.

Serving Ideas
A classic accompaniment is boiled potatoes.

SERVES 4-6

CHORIZO SAUSAGES WITH PEAS AND MINT

Spicy sausages are a perfect foil for the mild flavor of peas
and the cooling tang of mint in this informal dish.

4 chorizos
4oz salt pork, finely diced
1 small onion, finely chopped
½ clove garlic, finely chopped
¾ cup white wine
¾ cup water
1 bay leaf
Pinch salt and pepper
2 tsps chopped fresh mint
1lb shelled fresh peas or frozen peas

Step 3
Cook the onions
and garlic until
soft but not
colored.

Step 2
Cook the bacon
in its own fat until
crisp and golden
brown.

Step 4
Add all the
ingredients and
cook, uncovered,
until tender.

1. Place the chorizo sausages in a saucepan or frying pan and add enough water to cover completely. Bring to the boil and then reduce the heat to simmering. Cook, uncovered, for about 5 minutes and drain on paper towels. Set the sausages aside.

2. Cook the bacon slowly in a frying pan or saucepan until the fat is rendered. Then turn up the heat and cook until crisp and golden brown. Place on paper towels to drain.

3. Add the onion and garlic to the bacon fat in the pan and

cook until the onions are softened but not browned. Add the wine, water, bay leaf, bacon, mint, salt and pepper. Bring to the boil over high heat and then reduce to simmering. Add the sausages and cook, partially covered, for about 20 minutes.

4. If using fresh peas, add with the sausages. If using frozen peas, add during the last 5 minutes of cooking time. Remove sausages and slice. Add to the peas and re-heat if necessary. Using a draining spoon, place a serving on each plate.

Cook's Notes

 Time
Preparation takes about 20 minutes, or slightly longer if shelling fresh peas. Cooking takes about 35 minutes.

Variation
Lima beans or green beans may be used instead of the peas.

 Serving Ideas
Serve as a side dish to meat, poultry or fish. Add rice to serve as a main course.

SERVES 4

SWEETBREADS WITH PEPPERS AND SHERRY

Rich, velvety sweetbreads are perfectly complemented
by the sweet-sour taste of honey and vinegar.

2.2lbs lamb or calf sweetbreads
1 slice lemon
1 small red pepper, seeded and sliced
1 small green pepper, seeded and sliced
1 medium onion, peeled and thinly sliced
2 tbsps olive oil
1 tbsp butter or margarine
4 tbsps dry sherry
2 tbsps tarragon vinegar
1 cup chicken or veal stock
1 tbsp lemon juice
2 tbsps clear honey
Salt and pepper

1. Soak the sweetbreads in enough water to cover with the lemon slice for at least 2 hours. Transfer the sweetbreads to a saucepan and pour over clean water to cover.

2. Bring to the boil and cook for 10 minutes. Drain the sweetbreads and rinse them under cold water. Place drained sweetbreads on a plate and cover with another plate to weight down slightly. Leave to stand for 15 minutes.

3. Using a small, sharp knife, peel away the outer membrane from the sweetbreads.

4. Heat the oil, add the butter and, when foaming, fry the sweetbreads until golden brown. Remove them to a plate.

5. Cook the peppers and onions until softened and set them aside with the sweetbreads. Pour off any remaining fat in the pan.

6. Add the sherry and vinegar to the pan and boil. Pour on the stock and boil rapidly to reduce by half. Add the lemon juice and honey and return the sweetbreads and vegetables to the pan. Heat through and serve immediately.

Step 1
Soak the sweetbreads with a slice of lemon in enough cold water to cover.

Step 2
Once the sweetbreads have boiled, place them between two plates to weight down slightly.

Step 3
Use a small, sharp knife to pull away the outer membrane from the sweetbreads to keep them from shrinking and toughening.

Cook's Notes

Time
Preparation takes about 45 minutes, with 2 hours soaking time for the sweetbreads. Cooking takes about 25 minutes.

Preparation
The method for preparing sweetbreads is designed to allow the outer membrane to be removed fairly easily. This prevents the sweetbreads from shrinking and toughening.

Buying Guide
Sweetbreads are the thymus or pancreas of lambs and calves. Lamb sweetbreads are more readily available and are less expensive. Sweetbreads have a mild flavor much like chicken.

SERVES 6

PORK WITH TOMATO AND BLACK OLIVE SAUCE

A recipe like this one is often served in a small amount
as one of a selection of tapas − hors d'oeuvres.

3lb pork tenderloin, cut into ½ inch slices
Salt and pepper
4 tbsps flour
3 tbsps olive oil
1 medium-sized onion, thinly sliced
1lb canned tomatoes, drained and juice reserved
6 tbsps white wine
¾ cup light stock
3 slices cooked ham, shredded
1 hard-boiled egg
10-12 black olives, pitted and sliced
2 tbsps chopped parsley or coriander

Step 1
Place pieces of pork in a sieve with the flour and shake to coat evenly.

1. Mix the salt and pepper with the flour and coat the pieces of meat lightly, shaking off the excess. Heat the oil in a large frying pan and fry the meat, in several batches, until brown on both sides. Transfer the meat to a plate.

2. Add the onions to the pan and cook for about 5 minutes over low heat to soften but not brown. Add the tomatoes, wine and stock to the pan and bring to the boil.

3. Return the meat to the pan, cover and cook over low heat for about 30-40 minutes or until the meat is tender. Check the level of liquid and add some reserved tomato juice if necessary.

4. Cut the hard-boiled egg in half and remove the yolk. Cut the white into thin shreds. Five minutes before the end of cooking time, add the ham, egg white, olives and parsley to the sauce.

5. To serve, place pork slices on individual plates or on a large serving dish and spoon over the sauce. Push the egg yolks through a metal sieve to garnish the top of the pork. Serve immediately.

Step 2
Cook the onions until soft, but not colored.

Step 5
Push egg yolk through a sieve to garnish the pork.

Cook's Notes

Time
Preparation takes about 25 minutes and cooking takes about 30-40 minutes.

Serving Ideas
Serve with rice or potatoes and a green vegetable.

Buying Guide
Pitted black olives are available in delicatessens and large supermarkets.

SERVES 4

SHERRIED PORK WITH FIGS

Another popular Spanish fruit and meat combination.
Figs look especially attractive as a garnish and
really complement the sherry sauce.

2lb pork tenderloin
3 tbsps butter or margarine
1 bay leaf
1 sprig fresh thyme
½ cup medium-dry sherry
1 cup brown stock
Juice and zest of 1 large orange
1½ tbsps cornstarch
Pinch cinnamon
Salt and pepper
4 fresh figs

1. Slice the pork diagonally into pieces about ½ inch thick. Melt the butter or margarine in a large sauté pan and, when foaming, place in the slices of pork. Cook quickly on both sides to brown.

2. Pour away most of the fat and add the sherry. Bring to the boil and cook for about 1 minute. Pour on the stock and add the bay leaf and thyme. Bring to the boil and then lower the heat, cover and simmer for about 30 minutes or until the pork is tender.

3. When the pork is cooked, remove it from the pan and boil the liquid to reduce slightly. Add the orange zest to the liquid and mix the juice and cornstarch together. Spoon in a bit of the hot liquid and then return the mixture to the pan. Bring to the boil, whisking constantly until thickened and cleared. Stir in a pinch of cinnamon, salt and pepper. Return the pork to the pan and cook to heat through.

4. If the figs are small, quarter them. If they are large, slice lengthwise. Remove the pork to a serving dish and spoon over the sauce. Garnish with the sliced or quartered figs.

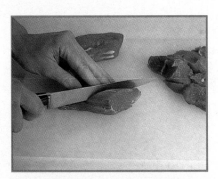

Step 1
Slice the pork tenderloin into diagonal pieces about 1/2 inch thick.

Step 1
Use a large sauté pan or frying pan to brown the slices of pork on both sides.

Step 3
Cook the pork over moderate heat until tender to the point of a knife. Do not allow the pork to boil rapidly.

Cook's Notes

Time
Preparation takes about 25 minutes and cooking takes about 45 minutes.

Preparation
Pork tenderloin can toughen if cooked too rapidly or over heat that is too high. Simmer gently in the liquid.

Serving Ideas
Serve with rice, either saffron or plain.

SERVES 4

PEPPERED FILLET OF LAMB WITH FRUIT

In Catalonia, on the border with France,
meat cooked with fruit is extremely popular.

2¼lbs lamb neck fillets
1 tbsp coarsely crushed black peppercorns
8oz dried fruit salad
4 tbsps butter or margarine
2 tbsps flour
1 cup light stock
½ cup medium dry sherry
3 tbsps heavy cream
Pinch salt
Coriander leaves to garnish

brown slightly. Stir in the stock gradually to blend well and add the sherry. Bring to the boil.

5. Drain the fruit, add to the pan and return the lamb fillets. Cover and cook over gentle heat for about 15-20 minutes or until lamb and fruit are tender.

6. When the lamb is cooked, remove it from the pan and slice into diagonal pieces about ¼ inch thick. Arrange on a serving plate and add the cooked fruit.

7. Add the cream to the sauce and bring to the boil. Allow to boil 1 minute to thicken and cook the cream and spoon the sauce over the fruit and meat to serve.

Step 2
Press the peppercorns firmly into the surface of each lamb fillet using your hand, a meat mallet or rolling pin.

Step 3
Fry the lamb fillets in a sauté pan or frying pan to brown evenly on all sides.

1. Place the fruit salad in a saucepan, cover with water and bring to the boil. Once the water boils, remove from the heat and leave to soak for about 2 hours.

2. Sprinkle the black peppercorns on the lamb fillets and press them in firmly with the palm of your hand, or bat them lightly with a meat mallet or rolling pin.

3. Melt the butter or margarine in a large sauté pan and when foaming, add the lamb fillets. Cook over moderately high heat to seal on both sides. When the lamb fillets are brown, remove them to a plate and set them aside.

4. Add the flour to the pan and cook over moderate heat to

Step 6
When lamb is cooked, slice it thinly on the diagonal.

Cook's Notes

Time
Preparation takes about 25 minutes, with 2 hours soaking time for the fruit. Cooking takes about 30-40 minutes.

Variation
Substitute pork tenderloins or fillet steaks for the lamb neck fillet. Lamb chops may also be used. Any combination of dried fruit may be used in this recipe.

Preparation
When coating the fillets with peppercorns, press firmly so that they stick well in the surface and do not fall off during cooking.

SERVES 4

CHICKEN WITH SAFFRON RICE AND PEAS

Saffron is frequently used in Spanish recipes. While it is expensive,
it gives rice and sauces a lovely golden color and delicate taste.

2 tbsps oil
2-3lb chicken, cut into 8 pieces and skinned if desired
Salt and pepper
1 small onion, finely chopped
2 tsps paprika
1 clove garlic, crushed
8 tomatoes, peeled, seeded and chopped
10oz rice
2½ cups boiling water
Large pinch saffron or ¼ tsp ground saffron
6oz frozen peas
2 tbsps chopped parsley

1. Heat the oil in a large frying pan. Season the chicken with salt and pepper and place it in the hot oil, skin side down first. Cook over moderate heat, turning the chicken frequently to brown it lightly. Set the chicken aside.

2. Add the onions to the oil and cook slowly until softened but not colored.

3. Add the paprika and cook about 2 minutes, stirring frequently until the paprika loses some of its red color. Add the garlic and the tomatoes.

4. Cook the mixture over high heat for about 5 minutes to evaporate the liquid from the tomatoes. The mixture should be of dropping consistency when done. Add the rice, water and saffron and stir together.

5. Return the chicken to the casserole and bring to the boil over high heat. Reduce to simmering, cover tightly and cook for about 20 minutes. Remove chicken and add the peas and parsley. Cook a further 5-10 minutes, or until rice is tender. Combine with the chicken to serve.

Step 3
Add the paprika and cook until it loses some of its red color.

Step 4
When the garlic and tomatoes are added, cook over a high heat to evaporate the liquid until the mixture is of a dropping consistency.

Step 5
Stir in the peas and parsley and cook for five minutes.

Cook's Notes

Time
Preparation takes about 20-25 minutes and cooking takes about 25-35 minutes.

Variation
If using fresh peas, allow about 14oz of peas in their pods. Cook fresh peas with the rice and chicken.

Serving Ideas
This is a very casual, peasant-type dish which is traditionally served in the casserole in which it was cooked.

SERVES 4

SPRING CHICKENS WITH BITTER CHOCOLATE SAUCE

A small amount of unsweetened chocolate lends a rich depth of color
and a delightfully mysterious flavor to a savory sauce.

4 tbsps olive oil
4 Rock Cornish hens
Salt and pepper
3 tbsps flour
1 clove garlic, crushed
1 cup chicken stock
4 tbsps dry white wine
2 tsps unsweetened cooking chocolate, grated
Lemon slices to garnish

Step 2
Cook the flour in
the oil until it turns
a pale straw color.

Step 1
Brown the hens in
the hot oil, turning
carefully to avoid
tearing the skin.

Step 5
Stir the grated
chocolate into the
sauce and cook
over low heat to
melt it.

1. Heat the oil in a heavy-based pan or casserole. Season the hens and place them, breast side down first, in the hot oil. Cook until golden brown on all sides, turning frequently.

2. Transfer the hens to a plate and add flour to the casserole. Cook until a pale straw color.

3. Add the garlic and cook to soften. Pour on the stock gradually, mixing well. Add the wine and bring to the boil.

4. Reduce to simmering, replace the hens and cover the casserole. Cook 20-30 minutes, or until the hens are tender.

5. Transfer the cooked hens to a serving dish and skim any fat from the surface of the sauce. Add the grated chocolate and cook, stirring quickly, over low heat for 2-3 minutes. Pour some of the sauce over the hens and garnish with lemon slices. Serve the rest of the sauce separately.

Cook's Notes

Time
Preparation takes about 20 minutes, cooking takes about 25-35 minutes.

Buying Guide
Unsweetened baking chocolate is not the same as semi-sweet chocolate, which must not be used as a substitute. Unsweetened chocolate is available in large supermarkets and specialty shops.

Serving Ideas
Serve with rice and a vegetable such as peas or asparagus, or with a green salad.

SERVES 4

VEAL WITH PEACHES AND PINENUTS

This dish is quite expensive, but very easy
and quick to prepare and cook.

4 ripe peaches
6 tbsps brandy or sherry
8 veal cutlets
Salt and pepper
½ cup dry white wine
Pinch cinnamon
1 small bay leaf
2 tbsps butter or margarine
4 tbsps pinenuts
1 tbsps cornstarch mixed with 2 tbsps water
Pinch sugar

1. Peel the peaches by dropping them into boiling water for about 30 seconds. Remove immediately to a bowl of cold water and leave to cool completely. Use a small, sharp knife to remove the peels.

2. Cut the peaches in half and twist the halves to separate. Remove the stones and place the peaches in a deep bowl with the brandy or sherry. Stir the peach halves to coat them completely.

3. Place the veal cutlets between 2 sheets of wax paper and use a rolling pin or meat mallet to bat out to flatten slightly. This may not be necessary. Heat the oil and fry the cutlets on both sides until golden brown. Pour on the wine and add the cinnamon, bay leaf, salt, pepper and cover the pan. Cook over low heat for about 15 minutes or until the veal is tender and cooked through.

4. While the veal is cooking, melt the butter in a small frying pan and add the pinenuts. Cook over moderate heat, stirring continuously until they are golden brown. Remove from the butter and set them aside to drain.

5. When the veal is cooked, remove it to a serving dish and keep it warm. Add cornstarch and water mixture to the pan and bring to the boil. Cook until thickened and cleared.

6. Remove the peaches from the brandy and slice them. Add the peaches and the brandy to the thickened sauce mixture and bring to the boil. Allow to cook rapidly for about 1 minute. Add the sugar, if using. Spoon the peaches and sauce over the veal cutlets and sprinkle on the browned pinenuts. Serve immediately.

Step 1
Place peaches in boiling water for 30 seconds.

Step 1
Transfer to cold water to cool completely – the peel will be easy to remove with a small knife.

Cook's Notes

Time
Preparation takes about 25-30 minutes, cooking takes about 25-30 minutes in total.

Variation
The recipe may be prepared with pork tenderloin, chicken breasts or duck breasts. Use nectarines or apricots instead of peaches and do not peel them.

SERVES 4

CHOCOLATE ALMOND STUFFED FIGS

A positively luxurious pudding that is deceptively easy to prepare. Try it when an elegant sweet is needed.

4 ripe figs
2 tbsps liquid honey
1 square unsweetened cooking chocolate
¾ cup ground almonds

Cinnamon Sauce

1 cup light cream
1 stick cinnamon
2 egg yolks
4 tbsps sugar
Ground cinnamon and blanched almond halves to
   garnish

1. Make a cross cut in each fig without cutting right down through the base. Carefully press the 4 sections of the fig out so that it looks like a flower.

2. Melt the honey and chocolate together over a very gentle heat in a small, heavy-based saucepan.

3. Set aside to cool slightly and then mix in the ground almonds.

4. When the mixture has cooled completely, spoon an equal amount into the center of each fig.

5. Meanwhile, prepare the sauce. Pour the cream into a deep saucepan and add the cinnamon stick. Bring just to the boil, draw off the heat and leave to infuse.

6. Beat the egg yolks and the sugar together until light, and gradually strain on the infused cream.

Step 6
Whisk egg yolks and sugar together until light.

Step 7
Combine cream and eggs and cook over gentle heat until mixture coats the back of a spoon.

7. Return the mixture to the saucepan and stir over gentle heat until it just coats the back of a spoon. Leave to cool until just warm.

8. To serve, pour some of the custard onto a serving plate and tilt the plate slowly to coat the base. Place a filled fig on top of the custard and sprinkle around some of the ground cinnamon, topping each fig with a blanched almond.

Cook's Notes

Time
Preparation takes about 20 minutes and cooking takes about 25 minutes.

Cook's Tip
While the custard is cooling, place a sheet of damp wax paper or plastic wrap directly onto the surface of the custard. This will prevent a skin from forming. Alternatively, leave out half of the sugar quantity and sprinkle the remainder over the top of the custard skin.

Preparation
Cook the custard over very gentle heat or in a double boiler to prevent curdling. If the custard should curdle, whisk vigorously or process in a food processor or blender and then strain.

MAKES 4 CUPS

Frozen Meringue Cream

This is a richer version of a typical
iced milk sweet found all over Spain.

4 cups light cream
⅓ cup sugar
1 whole vanilla bean
4 tbsps brandy
2 egg whites

Step 5
Whisk the egg whites until stiff but not dry and fold into the cooled cream mixture.

1. Combine the cream, sugar and vanilla bean in a deep, heavy-based saucepan.

2. Cook over very gentle heat for about 10 minutes, stirring frequently to dissolve the sugar. Do not allow the cream to boil.

3. Cover the pan and leave to infuse for about 15 minutes. Strain into a bowl to remove the vanilla bean and set aside to cool completely.

4. Beat the egg whites until stiff but not dry.

5. Fold them into the cooled cream mixture. Add brandy and chill completely.

Step 6
Freeze the cream mixture in shallow containers or ice cube trays until slushy.

Step 7
Mix with an electric mixer or in a food processor until the mixture is smooth, and then refreeze.

6. Pour into a shallow pan or ice cube tray and freeze until slushy.

7. Spoon the mixture into a food processor and work until smooth. Alternatively, use an electric mixer. Return the mixture to the freezer and freeze until nearly solid. Repeat the mixing procedure and then freeze in a rigid plastic container until firm. Allow the container to stand at room temperature for about 10 minutes before serving.

Cook's Notes

Time
Preparation takes about 20 minutes. Allow at least 2 hours for the freezing and mixing procedure.

Preparation
The freezing and mixing procedure eliminates large ice crystals from the sorbet. If desired, the sorbet may be processed again just before serving, but this will result in a very soft mixture.

Serving Ideas
Serve with chocolate sauce, fruit sauce or fresh fruit, cookies, or simply sprinkled with ground cinnamon or nutmeg.

SERVES 4-6

BANANA FRITTERS

Fritters, plain or made with fruit, are
a favorite sweet in Spain. Bananas are
especially nice prepared this way.

1 cup all-purpose flour, sifted
Pinch salt
¼ tsp ground cinnamon
1 egg, beaten
1 tbsp oil
⅓ cup milk
1 egg white, stiffly beaten
⅓ cup brandy or rum
2 tbsps sugar
1 tbsp lemon juice
6 ripe bananas, peeled and cut into sharp diagonal slices
    about ½ inch thick
Oil for frying
Powdered sugar

3. While the batter is resting, place the brandy or rum and sugar in a large bowl and stir well to help the sugar dissolve. Add the lemon juice and then slice the bananas. Place the bananas in the bowl, stirring to coat them completely. Set the bananas aside for about 20 minutes, turning them occasionally.

4. Heat the oil in a deep fat fryer or a large, heavy-based frying pan to a temperature of 375°F.

5. Dip the bananas in the batter using tongs or two forks. Drain off excess and fry a few pieces at a time in the hot fat. Drain on paper towels and sprinkle with powdered sugar before serving.

Step 2
When ready to use, fold in stiffly beaten egg white using a large metal spoon or rubber spatula.

Step 1
Mix the liquid ingredients in a well in the center of the flour, gradually drawing in the dry ingredients from the outside.

1. Sift half the flour with the salt and cinnamon into a large bowl and make a well in the center. Pour the beaten egg, oil and milk into the well and stir with a wooden spoon to gradually incorporate the flour from the outside. Stir just until the batter is smooth, but do not overbeat. Set the batter aside at room temperature for at least 30 minutes.

2. Whisk the egg white until stiff but not dry and fold into the batter just before ready to use.

Step 5
Dip the prepared banana slices into the batter using tongs or a fork. Allow the excess to drain away before frying.

Cook's Notes

Time
Preparation takes about 30 minutes and cooking takes about 2-3 minutes per batch of 5 or 6 fritters.

Preparation
When preparing batters for fritters or pancakes, it is best to let them stand for at least 30 minutes before using. This gives the batter a better consistency and makes it easier to use.

Variation
Pineapple, fresh or canned, or peeled apples may be used instead of the bananas.

MAKES 1 CAKE

Cinnamon Buttercream Cake

A cake that doesn't need baking is convenient any time, and perfect for summer. It's very rich, though, so it will go a long way.

1¼ cups sugar
1 cinnamon stick
⅓ cup water
8 egg yolks
1lb unsalted butter, softened
24 ladyfingers
⅓ cup brandy
¾ cup toasted almonds, roughly chopped
3oz semi-sweet chocolate, coarsely grated

1. Combine the sugar, water and cinnamon stick in a small, heavy-based saucepan and bring to the boil, stirring until the sugar dissolves.

2. Allow to boil briskly without stirring until the syrup reaches a temperature of 236°F on a sugar thermometer, or until a small amount dropped into cold water forms a soft ball.

3. While the sugar syrup is boiling, beat the egg yolks in a large bowl with an electric mixer until they are thick and lemon colored. Soften the butter until light and fluffy.

4. When the syrup is ready, quickly pour it in a thin, steady stream into the egg yolks, beating constantly with an electric mixer.

5. Continue beating until the mixture is thick, smooth and creamy. This will take about 10-15 minutes. Allow to cool to room temperature.

6. Beat in the softened butter, a spoonful at a time. Chill the mixture until it is of spreading consistency.

7. Cut the ladyfingers to fit closely together in an 8 inch square pan. Line the pan with lightly greased foil or paper.

8. Spread some of the buttercream lightly on one side of the ladyfingers and place them, powdered side down, in the pan. Cut small pieces of ladyfingers to fill in any corners, if necessary.

9. Sprinkle over half of the brandy, soaking each ladyfinger well. Spread over another layer of buttercream and place on the remaining ladyfingers, pushing them down to stick them into the cream. Sprinkle over the remaining brandy and cover the top with buttercream, reserving some for the sides. Place the cake in the refrigerator and chill until firm.

10. When the icing is firm, remove the cake from the refrigerator and lift it out of the pan using the foil or paper. Slide the cake off the paper onto a flat surface and spread the sides with the remaining buttercream. Press the chopped almonds into the sides and decorate the top with grated chocolate. Transfer to a serving dish and serve immediately.

Step 4
Pour the prepared syrup in a thin, steady stream onto the egg yolks while beating with an electric whisk.

Step 6
Beat in the softened butter, a spoonful at a time.

Cook's Notes

Time
Preparation takes about 45 minutes, with about 3 hours in the refrigerator to set the buttercream.

Variation
The icing may be flavored with 2 tsps instant coffee powder. Add when making the syrup.
2oz semi-sweet chocolate may be grated into the syrup once it is made and stirred to dissolve.

Preparation
The syrup must be at exactly the right temperature when it is beaten into the egg yolks or the icing will be soft and runny.

SERVES 8

CARAMEL CUSTARD WITH ORANGE AND CORIANDER

This is one of the best loved puddings in Spain. Fragrant coriander gives it
new appeal and its flavor is marvelous with orange.

6oz sugar
6 tbsps water
3 small oranges
3 cups milk
1 tbsp coriander seeds, crushed
6 eggs
2 egg yolks
6oz sugar

Step 1
Dissolve the sugar in water over gentle heat until it forms a clear syrup.

Step 2
Bring the syrup to the boil over high heat and watch carefully as it begins to turn brown.

1. To prepare the caramel, put the sugar and water in a heavy-based saucepan and bring to the boil over gentle heat to dissolve the sugar.

2. Once the sugar is dissolved, bring to the boil over high heat and cook to a golden brown, watching the color carefully.

3. While the caramel is cooking, heat 8 custard cups to warm them. When the caramel is brown, pour an equal amount into each cup and swirl quickly to coat the base and sides with caramel. Leave the caramel to cool and harden in the cups.

4. Grate the oranges and combine the rind, milk and crushed coriander seeds in a deep saucepan. Set the oranges aside for later use. Bring the milk almost to the boiling point and set it aside for the flavors to infuse.

5. Beat the eggs, yolks and sugar together until light and fluffy. Gradually strain on the milk, stirring well in between each addition. Pour the milk over the caramel in each cup. Place the cups in a bain-marie and place in a preheated 325°F oven for about 40 minutes, or until a knife inserted into the center of the custards comes out clean. Lower the oven temperature slightly if the water begins to boil around the cups.

6. When the custards are cooked, remove the cups from the bain-marie and refrigerate for at least 3 hours or overnight until the custard is completely cold and set.

7. To serve, loosen the custards from the sides of the cup with a small knife and turn them out onto individual plates. Peel the white pith from around the oranges and segment them. Place some of the orange segments around the custards and serve immediately.

Cook's Notes

Time
Preparation takes about 30-40 minutes, cooking time for the custards is about 40 minutes.

Watchpoint
The sugar and water can burn easily once it comes to the boil, so watch it carefully.

Preparation
A bain-marie literally means a water bath. To make one, pour warm water into a roasting pan, the level to come half way up the sides of the dish or dishes being used. This protects delicate egg custard mixtures from the direct heat of the oven. Check from time to time to see that the water is not boiling.

Cook's Tip
It is usual for some of the caramel to stick in the bottom of the dish when the custards are turned out. To make cleaning easier, pour boiling water into the bottom of each dish and leave until it dissolves the residue of caramel.

SERVES 6-8
FRIED MILK SQUARES

An unusual way with custard, this recipe requires
good organization for delicious results.

2 tbsps cornstarch
2½ cups milk
½ cup sugar
Vanilla extract
2 eggs, beaten
Dry breadcrumbs
Cinnamon sugar
Oil for deep frying

1. Place the cornstarch in a heavy-based saucepan and gradually whisk in the milk until completely blended. Add the sugar, stir well and bring the mixture slowly to the boil, stirring constantly until thickened. Stir in the vanilla extract.

2. Pour the mixture into an 8 inch square dish lined with lightly buttered foil.

3. Chill the mixture for at least 4 hours in a refrigerator, or until completely firm.

4. When set, lift out the paper and cut the mixture into squares with a knife dipped in hot water.

5. Coat the squares carefully with egg, using a fish slice.

6. Coat carefully with crumbs, patting them in place with your hands. Place the coated squares on a plate and set them aside.

7. Heat the oil in a deep fat fryer or deep saucepan and place in the squares, one at a time. Brown for about 2 minutes per side, turning over carefully. Drain on paper towels and transfer to a serving dish. Repeat with remaining squares. Sprinkle with sugar and cinnamon and serve immediately.

Step 4
When set, cut through the mixture with a knife dipped in hot water.

Step 5
Coat the squares carefully with beaten egg.

Step 6
Place crumbs on a sheet of paper. Use paper to toss the crumbs over the egg-coated squares.

Cook's Notes

Time
Preparation takes about 25 minutes, with 4 hours chilling time. Cooking takes about 4 minutes or longer if the squares are cooked in several batches.

Preparation
The milk mixture must be chilled until very firm before slicing. The squares must be completely cold before frying or they will begin to melt and fall apart. Using a knife dipped in hot water makes it easier to slice cleanly through the mixture.

Serving Ideas
The fried milk squares may be served with cream, either pouring or whipped. Fresh fruit such as strawberries, raspberries or sliced peaches make a nice accompaniment.

SERVES 4-6

SANGRIA

This is the ideal drink with hors d'oeuvres
on warm summer evenings and the perfect complement
to the flavor of Spanish food anytime.

4-6 tbsps sugar
1 lime
1 orange
1 lemon
4 tbsps brandy
1 bottle dry red wine
Soda water or sparkling mineral water
Ice cubes

Step 1
Slice the fruit
thinly and place in
a bowl or jug with
the sugar.

1. Slice the lime and lemon into rounds about ¼ inch thick.
Remove any pips.

2. Slice the oranges in half and then cut each half into ¼
inch thick slices, removing any pips. Place all the fruit in a
large bowl or jug.

3. Add the sugar, brandy and wine and stir until well mixed.
If desired, add a bit more sugar to taste.

4. Refrigerate the mixture for about 1 hour or until
thoroughly chilled. Chill the soda or mineral water separately. Just before serving, pour in the soda or mineral water,
adding about 2½ cups. Pour over ice into large wine
glasses, adding some of the sliced fruit to each glass, and
serve immediately.

Step 3
Add the wine and
brandy and mix
all the ingredients
to help dissolve
the sugar.

Step 4
Just before
serving, pour in
soda water or
carbonated
mineral water.

Cook's Notes

Time
Preparation takes about 20
minutes, with 1 hour chilling
time.

Cook's Tip
If Sangria is made more than
an hour or two in advance, the
fruit may discolor slightly because of
the wine. This will not affect the taste,
but fresh fruit may be substituted for
serving.

Variation
May also be made with dry
white wine.

SERVES 8

SPANISH LEMONADE

Spanish lemonade has a definite
kick, with the unusual combination
of both red and white wines.

¾ cup sugar
6 lemons
1 quart dry red wine
1 quart dry white wine
Fresh mint

Step 2
Slowly heat the
peel, sugar and
lemon juice, stirr-
ing occasionally
to dissolve the
sugar.

Step 1
Remove the peel
from the lemons
in thin strips,
using a serrated
knife or a
vegetable peeler.
Do not remove
the white pith.

Step 3
Add the lemon
slices and the
other ingredients
and pour into a
glass serving jug.

1. Place the sugar in a heavy-based saucepan. Peel the
rind carefully from three of the lemons using a sharp
serrated knife or a vegetable peeler. Do not take any of the
white pith off with the peel. Squeeze the lemons for juice
and strain them into the saucepan.

2. Place the saucepan over gentle heat to dissolve the
sugar, stirring occasionally. Set aside to cool completely.

3. Slice the remaining lemons about ¼ inch thick. Mix all the

ingredients together and pour into a large glass jug. Refrigerate for at least 4 hours or overnight, stirring occasionally.

4. Add just the leaves or small sprigs of mint to the lemonade, stirring them in well. To serve, pour into tall glasses over
ice.

Cook's Notes

Time
Preparation takes about 20
minutes with overnight chilling
time.

Variation
Use 7 or 8 limes or 3 oranges
in place of the lemons.

Preparation
Taste and add more sugar, it
necessary, before chilling the
lemonade.

INDEX

ACKNOWLEDGMENT
The publishers wish to thank the following suppliers
for their kind assistance:
Corning Ltd for providing Pyrex and other cookware.
Habasco International Ltd for the loan of basketware.
Stent (Pottery) Ltd for the loan of glazed pottery oven-
to-table ware.

Compiled by Judith Ferguson
Photographed by Peter Barry
Designed by Philip Clucas and Sara Cooper
Recipes Prepared for Photography by
Jacqueline Bellefontaine